Yo
Just Car

Poems of Family Life

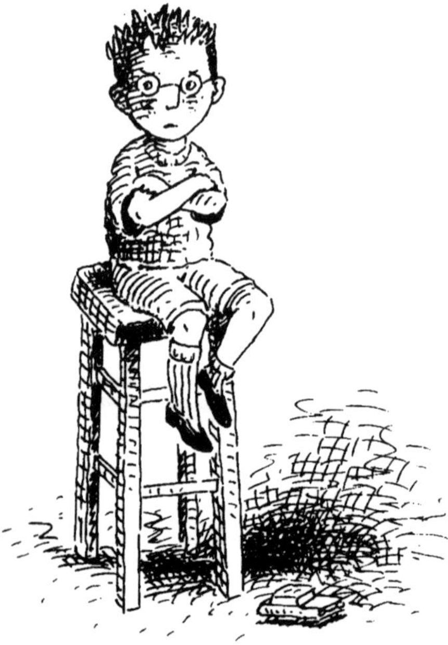

You Just Can't Win

Poems of Family Life

Selected by Brian Moses

Illustrated by Adriano Gon

Blackie

For Anne and Karen

Copyright © 1991 Brian Moses in this collection
Illustrations © 1991 Adriano Gon
First published 1991 by Blackie and Son Ltd

All rights reserved. No part of this publication may be reproduced, stored in a retrieval system, or transmitted in any form or by any means, electronic, mechanical, photocopying, recording or otherwise without the written permission of the Publishers.

A CIP catalogue record for this book is available from the British Library.

ISBN 0 216 93164 9 (hardback)
ISBN 0 216 93167 3 (paperback)

Blackie and Son Ltd
7 Leicester Place
London WC2H 7BP

Printed in Great Britain by
Thomson Litho Ltd, East Kilbride, Scotland.

Introduction

My small daughter Karen has just about sorted out who's who in our family. 'My grandma is your mum,' she says, or 'that's mum's mum,' or, 'she's mum's sister'. We hold sorting sessions where relatives are arranged, rearranged and then fitted together like pieces of a puzzle.

I can remember doing something similar with clouds as they floated over the gasworks. 'That's Uncle Bert and that's Aunt Lil, and that smaller cloud is their son John.' Why clouds? I've no idea, but it seemed to help with identification!

Someone once said that you can choose your friends, but you're stuck with your relations. No sooner do you start to recognise who's who in the family than some problem blows up and everyone chips in with their point of view. It's a battleground sometimes and everyone knows best, everyone that is except you! All the usual problem areas – television, homework, pets, manners, unsuitable friends, tidying up – you can argue, complain, shout, stamp, snipe, refuse to budge but adults are so unreasonable. They always know best, or so they say, but the annoying truth of the matter is that they often do! You end up tying yourself in knots trying to prove a point of view that you'd lost before you began.

Grandad is there with his, 'When I was a lad ...', Aunt Edie with, 'We never let our Joe behave like that ...', while Mum and Dad tell you how badly you're letting them down. Then brother and sister join in too, out to score points at your expense. You're rolled around like a ball in a pinball machine, nowhere to hide and at the mercy of everyone's whim. You might as well call it a day, go along with what they want. You know, you just can't win!

The poems in this book may not provide you with any answers but it helps sometimes to know that you're not the only one with problems. Perhaps when you read these poems you will discover situations that you recognise – a new baby in the house, a fight with brother or sister, being teased by Uncle Ken. There are poems that serve as portraits, Peter Dixon's 'mince pie of a mum', Berlie Doherty's 'prickle-chin dad', Ian Souter's grandpa, 'round-shouldered as a question-mark'. Some poems focus on the sad events that families have to live through, others will raise a smile or even make you laugh.

Parents, brothers, sisters, grans, grandads, aunts and uncles – when all is said and done, family ties are strong. As Tony Bradman says in his poem 'Alice':

>Little sister might be foul –
>But still, she's family.

BRIAN MOSES

Enter the Hero

'Were you born in a field?'
my mother yelled
as I left the door ajar.

'Put the wood in the hole!'
my old man growled
through a mouth like a gangster's scar.

But didn't they tell me
I'd been found
under a cabbage or goosegog tree,
squidgy as a little worm,
tall as a grasshopper's knee?

Because I looked a bit of a scruff,
not like a brand-new pin,
they tell me I am something
the dog has just dragged in!

Some days, some days, some days,
you know you just can't win.

MATT SIMPSON

Early to bed

The thing I can't stand
About grown-ups
Is the way
They say
You can't stay up late
To watch TV.
They make
You go off to bed
Then keep you awake
By watching themselves
Until midnight,
While you're lying in bed
With the noise
Of the programmes
Drumming through your head.

    Then, next morning,
    When you're yawning
    Because you couldn't get to sleep,
    And they're being crabby
    From staying up too late
    To watch TV,
    They say,
    'There you are, you see,
    You stayed up too late
    Watching TV.
    It's early to bed
    For you tonight.'
    Then, they rush off to work,
    Thinking they're right!

    JOHN FOSTER

This Time

I'm always doing things wrong,
I never get them right.
My sister always laughs
and that's when we start to fight.
We wrestle in the living-room,
I chase her up the stairs,
she flings the door in my face
and I ROAR like an angry bear.
Inside her room she's hiding
but I know just where she'll be,
crouched inside her wardrobe
waiting to jump out on me.
Then Dad calls out, *If you can't behave,*
I've told you what we'll do,
we'll go away for a holiday
and we won't be taking you.
Your Mum and I are tired
of your squabbles around the home,
if we leave you here together,
you'll have to get by on your own.
My sister comes out of the wardrobe
and we kneel by the bedroom door:
'Do you think they really mean it?'
'I don't know, I couldn't be sure.'
If you think we don't really mean it,
Dad shouts, *then just you step out of line.*
We look at each other, both thinking the same,
they really must mean it, this time!

BRIAN MOSES

Lisa's Protest

My mum's borrowed my mountain bike
to pop to the shops for a minute or so
it will be hours before she gets back
she's jammed the gears so the going is slow.

And dad has borrowed my personal stereo
just while he's mowing the lawn
I bet it comes back only fit for a burial
the wires ripped out and the earphones torn.

My brother has borrowed my reading book
to roll his toy cars along
I expect it'll get all ripped and unstuck
and I'll be the one in the wrong.

I tried the same stunt on my dad last night
tried to borrow five pounds interest free.
He smiled, shook his head, turned out the light
said never a borrower nor lender be.

Why can't I have the same deal as the rest
if it's OK for Dad, Mum and the brother
why should the daughter get second-best
we should all be the same as each other.

I'll borrow my mother's best straw hat
use it at school for a frisbee
borrow my dad's new cricket bat
take it up to the park, score a century.

I'll borrow my brother's crayons and stencils
make a big sign all about me
A Fair Deal For Lisa in bright coloured pencils
Fair Shares All Round In This Family.

DAVID HARMER

Wilde By Name ...

Cosmo's weird and Billy's naughty,
Jacky's odd and Jenny's rude,
Baby Mandy's just plain dirty –
They're a terrible lot, that wild Wilde brood.

Their dad won't work, he goes to the boozer,
Or hammers away out there in his shed.
Their mum won't cook, she goes to the chippy,
And when she wants to, stays in bed.

Their neighbours say that they're disgraceful,
They'd report them, if they dare.
The funny thing is – they seem quite happy.
I sometimes wish that I lived there.

JENNIFER & GRAEME CURRY

Things they say

Grow up girl.
Tidy your room.
Don't shuffle under the table.
Put the cat down
and don't kick the dog.
Don't give me that stuff, it's a fable.

Don't eat that plum.
Where are your manners?
Go, now, and see Mrs Brown.
Get down the shops
and buy me some tights
and don't hang around in the town.

I've told you before
and how many times
must I tell you to empty that bin?
Don't open that door
and don't close that window. . .
Just wait till your father gets in.

Grow up girl.
Tidy your room
or you won't see that game on TV.
If those things aren't away
when I come up again
you'll have to answer to me.

FRED SEDGWICK

The Pleasures of Family Conversation

Who spilled this milk?
I swear you're gonna cop it.

Just you get cracking
get a cloth and mop it.

And move that dish
don't you dare drop it.

Whose is this balloon
I swear I'm gonna pop it.

So move these toys
and just you stop it.

Get out of my sight
shove off, just hop it.

JOHN RICE

Ties

Father, mother,
Sister, brother,
Tied one to all,
Each to each other.

Ties that bind
Like solid steel,
Ties you can't see,
Only feel.

Travel far
And then you'll know
Ties that bind
And won't let go.

Father, mother,
Sister, brother,
Tied one to all,
Each to each other.

TONY BRADMAN

Dad

Dad is the dancing-man
The laughing-bear, the prickle-chin,
The tickle-fingers, jungle-roars,
Bucking bronco, rocking-horse,
The helicopter roundabout
The beat-the-wind at swing-and-shout
Goal-post, scarey-ghost,
Climbing-Jack, humpty-back.

But sometimes he's
A go-away-please!
A snorey-snarl, a sprawly slump
A yawny mouth, a sleeping lump,

And I'm a kite without a string
Waiting for Dad to dance again.

BERLIE DOHERTY

Daddy In Bed

When Daddy was in bed
It was very early.
He didn't wake up
So I shouted at him,
He still didn't wake up
So I jumped on him,
He still didn't wake up
So I pulled the quilt off him,
He still didn't wake up
So I tickled his feet,
He still didn't wake up
So I wiped him with a wet sponge,
He still didn't wake up
So I sprayed him with perfume,
He still didn't wake up
But he smelled nice.

NATASHA GAMMON (6)

Crazy

Dad says I'm crazy,
I don't see why he should –
What's wrong with liking lemonade
Poured on my Yorkshire pud?

CLIVE WEBSTER

My Mum

My Mum was a mince pie of a mum.
A 'doyouwantabiscuitwithyourtea?'
kind of mum.
A roast potato
   brown gravy
   crackle on the pork
   yorkshire pud
kind of lady.
She was a
   houseful of everyone
   polish the brass
   whiten the step
   rush to the shops
   bucket and mops
kind of lady.

A – 'hello dear'
     always near
     hurry scurry
'Oh, don't worry…'
kind of Mum.

She collected –
   old people
   funny stories
   and other people's children.

She called everyone by an invented name
and was a champion
     bus waiter
     queuer
     visitor
     laugher
     and Nutall Mint sucker.

She was someone
who
would give anyone
her last mint.

PETER DIXON

Magic

She puts her hands in the sink – with each deft flick
another plate comes out clean – I can't understand this:
even saucers are awkward to me, take an age to wash.
It's the same with flour: what runs and jumps from me
obeys her instantly, rolling itself into a neat ball
to unfurl like a handkerchief beneath her wand.
She says to the fire – go on, you, burn! – and it does.
Wool turns to clothes between her clicking fingers.
The hands are always moving, you seldom see the trick
till later, with surprise, you find the world changed:
the dust gone, the dress ironed, the food laid out to eat.
Clear up your toys – she says – they won't put themselves away;
but I think if she told them to, they would. She's so good
at that sort of magic.

Dave Calder

A Lesson for Mamma

Dear Mamma, if you just could be
A tiny little girl like me,
And I your mamma, you would see
   How nice I'd be to you.
I'd always let you have your way;
I'd never frown at you and say,
   'You are behaving ill today,
   Such conduct will not do.'

                 I'd always give you jelly-cake
                 For breakfast, and I'd never shake
                 My head, and say, 'You must not take
                    So very large a slice.'
                 I'd never say, 'My dear, I trust
                 You will not make me say you *must*
                 Eat up your oatmeal'; or 'The crust
                    You'll find, is very nice.'

I'd buy you candy every day;
I'd go down town with you, and say,
'What would my darling like? You may
   Have anything you see.'
I'd never say, 'My pet, you know
'Tis bad for health and teeth, and so
I cannot let you have it. No —
   It would be wrong in me.'

And every day I'd let you wear
Your nicest dress, and never care
If it should get a great big tear;
   I'd only say to you,
'My precious treasure, never mind,
For little clothes *will* tear, I find.'
Now, Mamma, wouldn't that be kind?
   That's just what *I* should do.

                    I'd never say, 'Well, just a *few*!'
                    I'd let you stop your lessons too;
                    I'd say, 'They are too hard for you,
                        Poor child, to understand.'
                    I'd put the books and slates away;
                    You shouldn't do a thing but play,
                    And have a party every day.
                        Ah-h-h! wouldn't that be grand!

But, Mamma dear, you cannot grow
Into a little girl, you know,
And I can't be your mamma; so
   The only thing to do,
Is just for you to try and see
How very, very nice 'twould be
For *you* to do all this for *me*,
   Now, Mamma, *couldn't* you?

SYDNEY DAYRE (MRS COCHRAN)

Lies

My father lied for me
when I refused to go to school
no special reason
except it was Monday
and raining
I blamed a headache but
he knew it wasn't true

He brought me aspirins
in a glass of water
said 'your mother would
have known what to do'
then I heard him phone
'there's been a spot of
trouble in the past

I'd like to let you know
today he's genuinely ill'
tea-time he asked me
'how are you now son?'
my head was thumping from
watching videos all day
'fine' I said 'just fine'

IRENE RAWNSLEY

DIVORCE

Dad's left. Is that right?

> Yes.
> It all
> centred
> on something
> Mum
> said.

So where does that leave you?

GINA DOUTHWAITE

The Shoes

These are the shoes
Dad walked about in
When we did jobs
In the garden,
When his shed
Was full of shavings,
When he tried
To put the fence up,
When my old bike
Needed mending,
When the car
Could not get started,
When he got up late
On Sunday.
These are the shoes
Dad walked about in
And I've kept them
In my room.

These are not the shoes
That Dad walked out in
When we didn't know
Where he was going,
When I tried to lift
His suitcase,
When he said goodbye
And kissed me,
When he left his door-key
On the table,

When he promised Mum
He'd send a postcard,
When I couldn't hear
His special footsteps.
These are not the shoes
That Dad walked out in
But he'll need them
When he comes back home.

JOHN MOLE

The New Baby

You really are lucky,
it is such a treat,
your new baby brother,
here for you to meet.

Sorry, but don't touch,
you'll poke out his eye.
Oh look now, your faces
have made baby cry.

> Don't make a noise now,
> baby's asleep.
> Turn off the TV,
> come and have a peep.
>
> Look at his little face,
> no, he's not dead.
> Don't tap his rattle,
> QUIET! I said

You've woken the baby.
Oh really, do try.
Why must you do things
that make baby cry?

Don't play trains dear,
put the spaceship away.
Yes, I am certain
that baby *will* stay.

ROBIN MELLOR

The First Tooth

Through the house what busy joy,
Just because the infant boy
Has a tiny tooth to show!
I have got a double row,
All as white, and all as small;
Yet no one cares for mine at all.
He can say but half a word,
Yet that single sound's preferred
To all the words that I can say
In the longest summer day.
He cannot walk, yet if he put
With mimic motion out his foot,
As if he thought he were advancing,
It's prized more than my best dancing.

CHARLES & MARY LAMB

New Baby

Mi baby sista come home las' week
An' little most mi dead,
When mama pull back de blanket
An' me see de pickney head.

Couple piece a hair she hab pon i'
An de little pickney face
Wrinkle up an crease up so,
It was a real disgrace.

Mi see har a chew up mama chest
So mi gi' har piece o' meat,
Mama tek i' whey, sey she cyaan eat yet
For she no hab no teeth.

Mi tell mama fi put har down
Mek she play wid mi blue van,
She sey Yvonne cyaan siddung nor stan' up yet
Nor hol' tings eena har han'.

Mi sey a' right but maybe
She can play 'I spy' wid mi,
She tell mi de pickney cyaan talk yet
An she can hardly see.

Aldoah she no hab no use,
An she always wet har bed,
Mi wouldn' mine so much ef she neva
Mek so much nize a mi head.

Every night she wake mi up;
But a mama mi sorry fah,
For everytime she wake up
She start fi eat mama.

She blind, she dumb, she ugly, she bald,
She smelly, she cyaan understan',
A wish mama would tek har back
An' buy one different one.

VALERIE BLOOM

My Brother is a Punk

My brother is a punk.
His hair stands in a spike.
He wears a torn-up jacket.
He rides a motorbike.

He makes a mess at table.
He gobbles down his food.
He often screams and shouts.
He walks round in the nude.

I'm glad that I'm not him
(I'm sure he must feel cold).
He really is a terror.
He's only two years old.

CHALRES THOMSON

Richard's Brother Speaks

Richard...
What's the matter? Why you not smiln' no more?
You wretch, you bruk the window?
Daddy a go peel you 'kin,
'Im a go peel it like how he peel orange.
When Daddy come true dat door
You better run.
You better leave de country!
'Im a-go peel you 'kin.
You bottom a go warm tonight though!
Me goin' cook dinner pon you backside
When 'im done wid you
Richard 'im a come!
Run, bwoy, run!

DESMOND STRACHAN

Brother Trouble

Wipe! Wipe! Wipe!
That's my brother wiping up.
He doesn't wipe he just sort of,
Waves at a plate.
'Finished,' he announces.
'What about those marks?' I ask.
'Shadows,' he replies, and turns the plate over.
'See you later, Washing Up Investigator – I'm off!'
And he does his Invisible man routine,

V   A   N   I   S   H   E   S

Then,
                        CRASH!
           CRASH!
CRASH!

As he becomes prehistoric man
Lumbering up the stairs.

THUD! THUD! THUD!

That's his,
'I'm tap dancing across my bedroom disguised
As an elephant' act.
Now it's

   I   I   I
O   N   O   N   O   N
B   G!   B   G!   B   G!

He's practising somersaults on his bed
BANG! BANG! CRASH!
Now he's *not* practising somersaults on his bed.
He's bouncing his head off the floor instead!
AAAGH! AAAGH! OOOH!
Now he'll start playing at doctors.
And guess who'll be the patient?
'Mum! MUM! **MUM!**'
What a noise.
His mouth's so big you could make
A triple-decker sandwich inside it.
Dear! Dear! Dear!
That's doctor mum off to the rescue.
Always smiling and always caring.
'Shame! Shame! Shame!'
She never really tells him off.
Just says he's an itsy bitsy bit of a pest.
Yes I agree
I suppose
Like a great big wasp,

STUCK UP MY NOSE!

IAN SOUTER

Favouritism

When we caught measles
It wasn't fair –
My brother collected
Twice his share.

He counted my spots:
'One hundred and twenty!'
Which sounded to me
As if I had plenty.

Then I counted his -
And what do you think?
He'd two hundred and thirty-eight,
Small, round and pink!

I felt I'd been cheated
So 'Count mine again!'
I told him, and scowled
So he dared not complain.

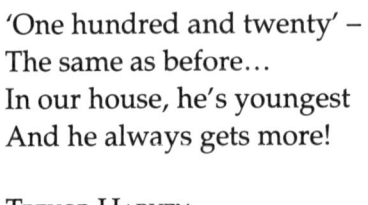

'One hundred and twenty' –
The same as before…
In our house, he's youngest
And he always gets more!

TREVOR HARVEY

Big and Little

We're so different in size
You'd hardly realise
We're related to each other,
But I'm the small girl with the big brother.

I'm the one on Sports Day
Who wriggles my way
Through the crowd of parents
Like Gulliver squeezing through the corn
In the land of the giants
To cheer my brother on.

When he scores the winning goal
I forget
It's wet
And my feet are cold.

But he's the one to shout
When at rounders I hit out
And people say 'There's another
As good at games as her brother!'

STANLEY COOK

Face-Pulling Contests

My sister and I
hold face-pulling contests.

I start with my
zombie at midnight look
while she hooks two fingers
into her mouth and pulls out
her sabre-tooth tiger scowl.

I try my curse
of the killer mummies,
but she rolls her eyes
and curls her lip,
sticks out her teeth
and pretends she's Drac.
I clutch at my throat
and finger a bolt,
then zap her with
Frankenstein's features.

She comes at me
with her wolf-woman sneer,
but I can howl
much better than her.
And now she's stuck
for something to do,
and this time I'm thinking
I'll beat her for sure
with my purple planet people eater…

when Mum steps in
to check the noise,
and no one pulls a better face
than Mum when she's annoyed.

My sister and I
are mere beginners:

Mum's the winner!

BRIAN MOSES

One Spring Day

Melanie, Melanie Wilberforce
Knows just how it feels
To clatter down the garden path
In her mam's high heels.

Baby brother, Charlie,
Is snoozing in his pram
Underneath the washing-line
Quiet as a lamb.

Clatter, crunch, clatter
Those spiky heels go,
Crunch, scrape, clatter, clack…
Little can she know

That Charlie's going to wake and bawl
Any minute now
And mum is going to dash outside
And make poor Melanie howl.

But until that awful moment comes
Let little Charlie snooze
And Melanie scrape the concrete
In her mam's best shoes.

This world is full of trouble,
So let the baby snore
And Melanie go a-clattering
Half a minute more.

MATT SIMPSON

Four Years Old – A Nursery Song

One cannot turn a minute,
But mischief – there you're in it,
A-getting at my books, John,
With mighty bustling looks, John;
Or poking at the roses
In midst of which your nose is;
Or climbing on a table,
No matter how unstable,
And turning up your quaint eye
And half-shut teeth with 'Mayn't I?'
Or else you're off at play, John,
Just as you'd be all day, John,
With hat or not, as happens,
and there you dance, and clap hands,
Or on the grass go rolling,
Or plucking flowers, or bowling,
And getting me expenses
With losing balls o'er fences;
And see what flow'rs the weather
Has render'd fit to gather;
And, when we home must jog, you
Shall ride my back, you rogue you.
Your hat adorn'd with fir-leaves,
Horse-chestnut, oak, and vine-leaves;
And so, with green o'er head, John,
Shall whistle home to bed, John.
– But see, the sun shines brightly;
Come, put your hat on rightly,
And we'll among the bushes,
And hear your friends the thrushes.

LEIGH HUNT

William

William!
Willie!!
Hey, Will! Stand still!
Why don't you do as you're told?
Let me tuck your shirt in,
You'll catch your death of cold.
Leave the sand in the sandpit
And don't bury the cat!
Put the gardening-shears away –
DON'T YOU DARE DO THAT!
Stay where I can see you
And don't climb any trees.
Get up off the garden;
Look at the state of those knees!
What have you got in your mouth?
Open it, let me see.
Where did you get that chewing-gum?
Give it to me!
Where is your new bike?
What? You've left it in the street?
Go and fetch it at once, young man,
Or that's your very last treat!
Hmm, I should think you *are* sorry,
You're lucky it was still there.
OK, yes you can clean it,
But just you take good care.
No, you don't need the hose-pipe,
I said no – PUT IT DOWN!
That wasn't very funny,
This is *not* a smile, it's a frown.
Right, I'm turning the water off!

Joke's over. I've had my fill.
William, *don't* do it again!
Willie!!
Will he?
He will!

RAY MATHER

Would You Believe It?

This morning
Me,
The teaser-pleaser, know-it-all brother,
Told my itchy-titchy, believe anything sister,
That sitting on her head was a flower-bed,
That covering her hair was a chocolate eclair,
That inside her ears were mountaineers,
That her eyes were made of apple pies,
That her arms had changed to fire alarms,
That on her bones were telephones,
That hanging from one knee was a cup of tea,
That her shorts were now tennis courts,
That her legs were smothered in fried eggs,
And that her toes were covered with pretty, pink bows.
Do you know she nearly believed me
And rushed off to the bathroom mirror to check!
My itchy-titchy, believe anything sister,
Won't be as much fun when she grows up.
So what will
Me,
This teaser-pleaser, know-it-all brother
Do then?

Ian Souter

Alice

Alice hates her sister,
She loathes with all her might,
For sisters are such know-it-alls,
Horrors full of spite.

> Alice hates her sister,
> Her parents' darling child;
> The way they simper over her
> Drives poor Alice wild.

Alice hates her sister,
At school it's just the same,
Little sister hangs around
And spoils big sister's games.

> Alice hates her sister,
> She'd like to do her in;
> She's such a nasty piece of work
> It wouldn't be a sin.

Alice hates her sister. . .
But wait – what's going on?
Little sister's howling now,
Something's very wrong.

> Alice hates her sister,
> But she hates a bully more,
> Which is why she bashes Billy,
> And lays him on the floor.

Alice hates her sister,
Though the moral's plain to see;
Little sister might be foul –
But still, she's family.

TONY BRADMAN

Sisters

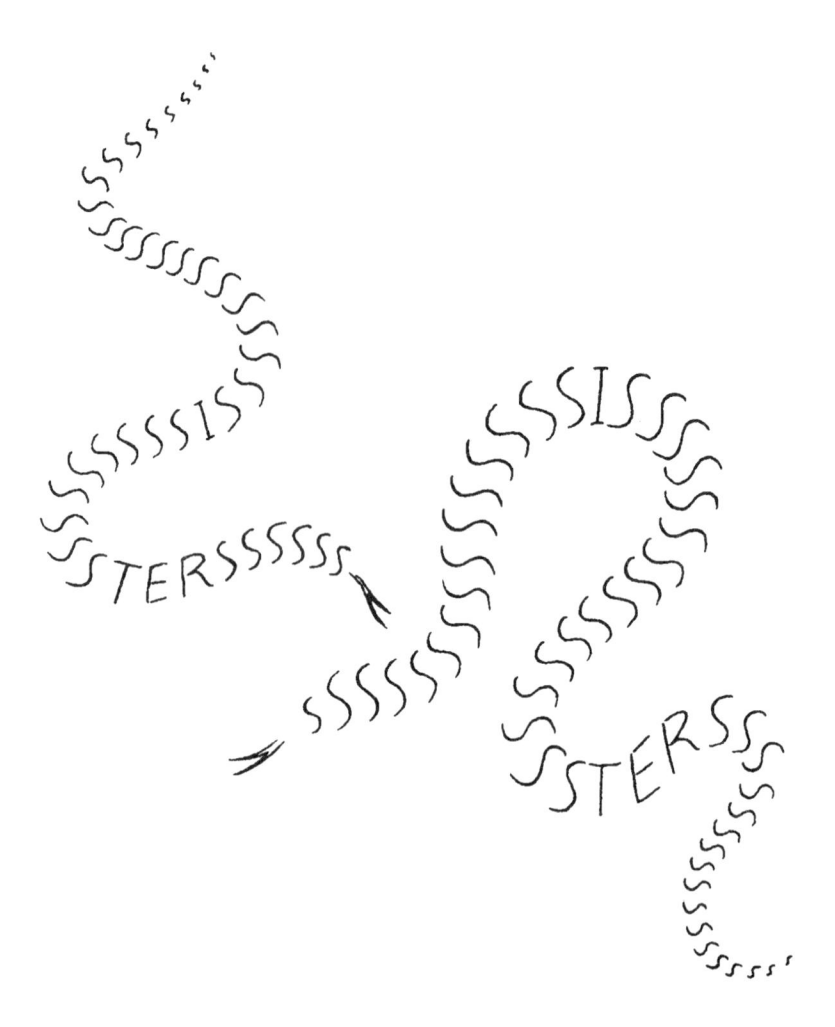

sssssss
sssssssss
ssssssssss
sssssis   ssssisss
sstersssss   sssssssssssss
         sssssssss sssssss
          ssterss
                ssssss
                 sssssss

Gina Douthwaite

Mima

Jemima is my name,
   But oh, I have another;
My father always calls me Meg,
   And so do Bob and mother;
Only my sister, jealous of
   The strands of my bright hair,
'Jemima—Mima—Mima!'
   Calls, mocking, up the stair.

WALTER DE LA MARE

My Little Sister

My sister
and I
always
fight.

I'm sure she's
wrong. I
think I'm
right.

                                      She pinches my
                                      toys
                                      when I'm not
                                      there

                                      she cheats at
                                      games.
                                      She's never
                                      fair.

She leaves her
clothes
all over the
place

if I
complain
she pulls a
face.

Every
morning
I have to
wait

to take her
to school…
we're always
late…

                              but however
                              naughty
                              she can
                              be

                              nothing
                              must hurt her.
                              She's smaller
                              than me.

                              Ann Bonner

Sister

Tell me a story!
Lend me that book!
Please, let me come in your den?
I won't mess it up,
so *please* say I can.
When? When? When?

Lend me that engine,
that truck - and your glue.
I'll give half of my old bubblegum.
You know what Dad said
about learning to share.
Give it *now* –
or I'm telling Mum!

Oh, *please* lend your bike –
I'll be careful this time.
I'll keep out of the mud
and the snow.
I could borrow your hat –
the one you've just got…

              said my sister.

And I said

              NO!

JUDITH NICHOLLS

Lively Lou and Lazy Lynn

Lively Lou and Lazy Lynn
Were each the other's identical twin
Each wore different coloured clothes
But they weren't as different as some supposed...

Lively Lou and lazy Lynn
One went out and the other stayed in
One got up and the other sat down
One gave a smile and the other gave a frown
One made her bed and the other made a mess
One wore jeans and the other wore a dress
One liked jam and the other liked cheese
Lazy Lynn and her twin Louise.

But sometimes just to cause confusion
They'd carry out a small illusion:
Lou stayed in and out went Lynn
Lou was quiet and Lynn made a din
Lou would scowl and Lynn would grin.
Is Lynn Lou or is Lou Lynn? Who knows
Which one is wearing which one's clothes?
So, when someone commits a little sin...
Well,
No one knows *which* identical twin.

TREVOR MILLUM

Sisters

Sally hasn't talked to me for ages.
   She shouts, she swears
   She sneers and jeers, she rages
   She stamps around and slams the door
But doesn't *talk*.
All she'll say to me these days is
'Get lost, go away,
Leave me *alone!*'

Sally hasn't laughed with me for ages.
   She doesn't smile
   Or grin or giggle,
   Won't share a joke.
And when I tell her something funny
She throws her eyes up to the ceiling
Says, as if to someone else:
'Why don't that stupid kid shut up!'

Sally hasn't played with me for ages.
   We used to get the doll's house out,
   Go skipping in the street, or
   To the playground in the park together.
But now, it's like it never happened,
She's trying to pretend
Even to me
She's never *played* with anything, not ever.

Sally hasn't wanted me for ages.
   She's getting too *grown-up*
   To be seen with me,
   She reckons.
But I can get my own back, don't you worry.
It's nearly bedtime and I've hidden
The teddy bear
She sleeps with every night.

(And in a little while we'll see
How grown-up my sister Sally
Really is ...)

Mick Gowar

One thing leads to another

My little sister told a lie
and she was found out, so she
cried, tears falling soft
as melting snow.
                Our mother
said that she was such a
bad little girl she'd have
to go to the old woman who
collects naughty children
in a basket.
                (And that was
another lie!)
                Our mother
lifted the telephone. 'Take
this child away,' she said.
My little sister threw
herself on the floor and
sobbed. I couldn't bear it
any longer.
                'Stop it, please
STOP IT!' I shouted. 'She's
frightened. She won't do it
ever again.'
                And our mother
showed me she had her hand
over the mouthpiece, but
my little sister didn't know
that and she cried like she'd
forgotten how to stop.
                So

I hit our mum, and I punched
her, and I kicked her. And
she got mad and yelled at me.

Quiet now, face puddled with
tears, my little sister stood
watching.
        I bet she didn't
even remember that she was
the one who started it all.

MOIRA ANDREW

Harry pushed her

Harry pushed her;
He pushed her around;
He pushed his sister.
Before school, after school;
On weekends.
He pushed his sister;
He had no friends.
He pushed her: school holidays
And Christmas time.
The children always
Sang their made-up rhyme:
'Harry push her! Push her quick!
Harry push her! Make her sick!'
Harry pushed her without strain:
Through snow, sunshine, wind and rain.
She smiled strangely
And never said a word.
He pushed her for years –
It was so absurd.
Harry was twelve;
His sister twenty-three.
Harry never had a childhood like me.
Harry pushed her without a care;
He pushed his sister in her wheelchair.

PETER THABIT JONES

Alone in the House

I like being left alone
When everyone's gone out.
I change from Channel 1 to 3
And from 3 to 4 to 2,
I play the music centre
As loud as it will go,
I call up Dial-a-Recipe
And talk back to the voice,
Search the fridge and larder
For leftover luxuries,
Put pickled onions and bananas
In my giant sandwiches,
I crunch the solid icy peas
Straight from the freezer tray
And write notes to our milkman
'Three hundred pints today'.
I creep round in the darkness
Pretending I'm a burglar or a cat,
I slither head first down the stairs
In my brother's sleeping bag
And I read the books my sister
Keeps hidden from my dad.
Then. . .
I sit down with my sandwich
In my father's favourite chair
Put my feet up on the table
And feel glad that they're not there
...once in a while.

TREVOR MILLUM

Mementoes

There's a place
in our garden
where the lawn's worn bare
by my goalie dives

and under the settee
in the front room
there's a pile
of Asterix books

                                      that are falling apart.
                                      In the bathroom
                                      there's talc
                                      in a bear-shaped bottle;

                                      and the kitchen cupboards
                                      are filled with things
                                      my parents never eat or drink:
                                      Appletize, tomato ketchup,

Cocopops, chocolate spread.
My drawings improve
the walls of our house
everywhere:

my monsters, my elephant,
my pyramids. Photos
abound, too
where my parents work.

Me on my second birthday,
me in the temple at Karnak,
making a face. Or running
after Oscar the dog. . .

When I sleep round Joe's
my parents look
at these things
and wish I was home

so I could ruin the lawn.
They look in my bedroom
in the morning
and say 'Shall I get him now?'

Then I am a prince
welcomed back to the kingdom.
I untidy things again
and de-silence the rooms.

FRED SEDGWICK

Unfair

They say I've got my father's nose
They say I've got his walk
And there's something about my grandad
In the serious way I talk.

'And aren't his legs just like our Jack's,'
Says smiling Auntie Rose
'He could bend them just like that
And touch his head with his toes.'

I've got Auntie Julia's funny laugh
I've sister Betty's lips
And just like Sid on my mother's side
I'm fond of fish and chips.

I have moods that remind them of Auntie Vi
And my hair's just like their Paul
Sometimes when I look in the mirror
I wonder if I'm me at all.

But what I ask myself is this
Why does it have to be
That it's me who looks like them and not
Them that looks like me.

GARETH OWEN

Well Caught

These days I'm in love with my face.
It has grown round and genial as I've become older.
In it I see my grandfather's face and that
Of my mother. Yes – like a ball it has been thrown
From one generation to the next.

GERDA MAYER

Advice

Do put a coat on,
and fasten that shoe.
I'd take a sweater,
    if I were you…

It's chilly at nights now,
you're bound to catch 'flu;
I'd button up warmly,
    if I were you…

Please yourself if you must
but I know what *I'd* do;
I'd stay at home now,
    if I were you…

The nights have drawn in,
you never know who
might be lurking out there
    just waiting for you…

I don't know what the youth
of today's coming to!
They do what they like
    and like what they do!

Now when *I* was young,
it caused hullaballoo
if I stayed out past nine –
  and I never dared to.

If I were young now,
I know what *I'd* do…

  I'd enjoy every minute
    if I were you!

JUDITH NICHOLLS

Poor Grandma

Why this child
so spin-spin spin-spin
Why this child
can't keep still

Why this child
so turn-round
turn-round
Why this child
can't settle down

Why this child
can't eat without getting
up to look through window
Why this child must behave so
I want to know
Why this child
so spin-spin spin-spin
Why this child
can't keep still

GRACE NICHOLS

My Grandpa

My grandpa is as round-shouldered as a question-mark
And is led about all day by his walking stick,
With teeth that aren't real,
Hidden behind a moustache that is,
While his memories simmer warmly
inside his crinkled paper bag of a face.
My grandpa,
Old and worn on the outside,
Sparky and fresh on the in.
For he often,
Shakes my hand with fifty-pence pieces,
Makes sweets pop out from behind his ears,
Smokes all day like a train
Then laughs like one as well.
Plays jokes on my mother
as he tries to freshen her face with a smile,
And then tells me stories that electrify my brain.
But best of all,
When my dad loses his temper,
Grandpa just tells him
TO SIT DOWN AND BEHAVE HIMSELF.
Good old grandpa.

IAN SOUTER

Birthdays

My dad says
Birthdays are like snow:
Something to look forward to
While you're little,
A nuisance
Once you've grown up.

My grandad says
That just means
He's jealous
Of me and my sledge.

KEVIN McCANN

Grandad's Birthday

Nineteen-O-nine
is a jolly long time.
Almost as long as Grandad's
Stories.

PETER DIXON

Thirteen Grandmas

I know a girl with thirteen grandmas –
one for her mum and twelve for her dad;
just think of Christmas or a birthday,
that many presents can't be bad.

But wait a moment, there's a problem,
thirteen times *thank-you* you'd have to write,
that many letters would take a weekend
and you'd be sticking on stamps all night.

On the other hand there are always the ice-creams
that grandmas buy children for a treat,
and sticky candy and jelly babies,
and everything else you like to eat.

But there'd be thirteen bags to carry
on the way home from the shop,
and thirteen *Now, when I was a girl,*
and other stories that never stop.

So I'll be satisfied with my grandmas
and I'll gladly give them due,
I get pretty well looked after,
even though I've got only two.

ROBIN MELLOR

Until Gran died

The minnows I caught
lived for a few days in a jar
then floated side-up on the surface.
We buried them beneath the hedge.
I didn't cry, but felt sad inside.

> I thought
> I could deal with funerals,
> that is until Gran died.

The goldfish I kept in a bowl
passed away with old age.
Mum wrapped him in newspaper
and we buried him next to a rose bush.
I didn't cry, but felt sad inside.

> I thought
> I could deal with funerals,
> that is until Gran died.

My cat lay stiff in a shoe box
after being hit by a car.
Dad dug a hole and we buried her
under the apple tree.
I didn't cry, but felt *very* sad inside.

> I thought
> I could deal with funerals,
> that is until Gran died.

And when she died
I went to the funeral
with relations dressed in black.
They cried, and so did I.
Salty tears ran down my face. Oh, how I cried.

   Yes, I thought
   I could deal with funerals,
   that is until Gran died.

She was buried in a graveyard
and even the sky wept that day.
Rain fell and fell and fell,
and thunder sobbed far away across the town.
I cried and I cried.

I thought
I could deal with funerals,
that is until Gran
died.

WES MAGEE

Grandpa

Grandpa's hands are as rough as garden sacks
And as warm as pockets.
His skin is crushed paper round his eyes
Wrapping up their secrets.

BERLIE DOHERTY

Good Advice

Wash yuh han dem before yuh eat
Sit still, stop twitching in yuh seat,
Don' bang the plate with yuh knife an fork,
An keep quiet when big people a-talk
Stop drag yuh foot dem pon the floor,
Ah tell yuh a'ready, don' slam the door,
Cover up yuh mout when yuh a cough,
Don' be greedy, give yuh sister half
O' the banana that yuh eating there,
What kind o' dress that yuh a-wear?
Don' hiss yuh teeth when me talk to yuh.
And mind how yuh looking at me too,
Teck me good advice me girl,
Manners carry yuh through the worl',
Ah tellin yuh this fe yuh own good
Yuh should thank me, show me some gratitude.

Life is really tough for me,
When Uncle Henry comes to tea.

VALERIE BLOOM

A Mystery

Where do aunties come from
It's a mystery to me.

They get off buses in the middle of the day
Land in your front room and then just stay.

They 'phone from faraway stations
Saying they'll be with you by eight.

They send postcards from Spain
When you didn't know they were away.

Where do aunties come from
It's a mystery to me.

Sometimes they arrive in twos
Take over the settee

They always keep their hats on
And balance brimming cups of tea

They scare your dad, they worry your mum
The dog and the cat have to leave home

Where do aunties come from
It's a mystery to me.

Then it's all over, quick as it began
Suitcase in the kitchen, coat back on.

It's been lovely, I must come again
Yes do says dad squeezing out a grin

They insist on a kiss, leave it on your cheek,
Bright red lipstick, it's there for a week.

Where do aunties come from
It's a mystery to me.

MARTIN WILEY

Aunt Sue's stories

Aunt Sue has a head full of stories
Aunt Sue has a whole heart full of stories.
Summer nights on the front porch
Aunt Sue cuddles a brown-faced child to her bosom
And tells him stories.

Black slaves
Working in the hot sun,
And black slaves
Walking in the dewy night,
And black slaves
Singing sorrow songs on the banks of a mighty river
Mingle themselves softly
In the flow of Old Aunt Sue's voice,
Mingle themselves softly
In the dark shadows that cross and re-cross
Aunt Sue's stories.

And the dark-faced child listening
Knows that Aunt Sue's stories are real stories.
He knows that Aunt Sue never got her stories
Out of any book at all,
But that they came
Right out of her own life.

The dark-faced child is quiet
On a Summer night
Listening to Aunt Sue's stories.

LANGSTON HUGHES

Afternoon Tease

Now we're sitting round the table,
now there's no chance of escape,
my Uncle Ken
(the worst of men)
will turn to me and say,
'What's her name then?'

Even though I know
he's going to say it
(he says it every time he
and Auntie Brenda come to tea)
I'm always unprepared.

'What's her name then?'

I'd like to come straight out with
'Her name's Ann'
but I go as pink as the leftover radishes,
feel as hot as the teapot
and choke on my trifle.

'Leave the boy alone,'
says Auntie Brenda,
'he's not old enough
to have a girlfriend,
are you, love?'

'Her name's Ann,' I mumble.
(My ears are on fire
but no one appears to notice).

Dad and Uncle Ken are discussing
yesterday's match
and Auntie Brenda
(far from slender)
is accepting another bowl
of rhubarb crumble
(with cream).

Having a meal with Uncle Ken
is an ordeal.

He makes me feel *this* small.

After he's gone
Mum will say,
'Take no notice,
he's only teasing you.'

BERNARD YOUNG

Cousin Janice with the Big Voice

When my cousin Janice
Opens her mouth to speak
A storm kindles behind her teeth
And a gale pours out.
This is a voice used
To holding conversations
With cows and sheep and dogs
Across mountains and valleys.
But here across the table-cloth
In our small flat
When she asks for the sugar
The teacups tremble
And a tidal wave foments
In the eddies of the cherry trifle.

GARETH OWEN

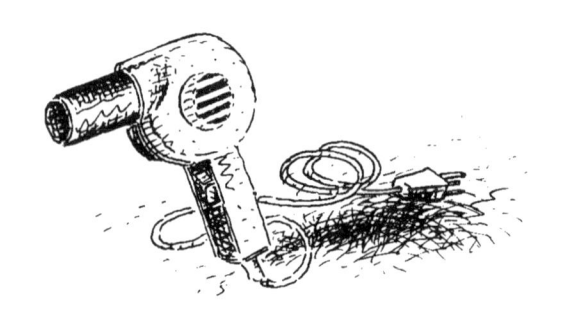

Nine Down

The cat's got run over,
Mum says...
                    and into my head soars the
                dead blackbird he dropped on
              the front door mat and the
         harvest mouse he secreted into my
      bedroom and the goldfish pawed out of
the pond one sunny afternoon and the spiders
    stalked across the kitchen floor and the
        times he got shut in Mrs. Moaner's
        garage by mistake and disgraced
himself in his fright and how he'd tightrope across the
top of the garden fence and leap up on the window
ledge and yowl to be let in and we'd argue about whose turn it
                              was to feed
            him and he'd headbutt your
        arm and make you spill the milk all
      over and sometimes he used to swipe the
      dog across her nose just because she'd
    dared to look at him and his warming lump
curled up purring on my morning duvet and inside my
                                      mind has
                                   splintered
                                         into
                                           a
                              myriad fragments
                                          of
                                         loss

IRENE YATES

It's a dog's life

Mum says
Our dog's
Having an identity crisis.

Yesterday,
He went out into the garden,
Then tried to come back in
Through the cat-flap.

He jammed his head so tight,
No matter how hard
We pushed and pulled
It wouldn't budge.

In the end,
We had to call the fire brigade.

When Dad came home
He nearly had a fit,
When he saw
What they'd done to the door.

He called the dog
All sorts of names.
But when the dog jumped up
To beg for his evening walk,
Dad still took him.

It's not fair.
If I'd smashed the door,
I wouldn't have been allowed out
For at least two weeks!

JOHN FOSTER

Gran's Green Parrot

It was high summer.
Age nine I travelled alone
to stay at Gran's.
'ello 'ello 'ello 'ello
screeched her green parrot
when I entered the front room
and gazed up at the huge cage
perched high on a wooden pedestal.

That amazing parrot!
Its shrill whistle
could pierce your eardrum.
It scattered sunflower seeds
half-way across the carpet
and then climbed around
and around its cage
cackling like a crackpot!

'oo's that? 'oo's that?
it squealed when my father
arrived to take me home.
Just watch this, said Dad,
and poked his finger at the cage.
The parrot raced along its perch
and flew at him in a rage.
Dad's finger jabbed closer, closer.

Furious, Gran's green parrot shrieked
at that teasing finger
until, like lightning,
it struck at Dad's flesh.
That black beak. . .wearing blood-red lipstick!
Dad tore around and around
Gran's front room
hollering like a hooligan!

WES MAGEE

Wildlife

Our back garden swarms with cats
the street is full of snarling dogs
more vicious than a pack of wolves
it's like a zoo round here.

Next door they've got a cockatiel
and several sorts of bright blue budgies
my dad stuffs his loft with pigeons
it's like a zoo round here.

Beside our pond that teems with fish
the guinea-pigs and rabbits live
in hutches stacked like high-rise flats
it's like a zoo round here.

I've got two gerbils and a hamster
my brother Joe keeps five white mice
my baby sister's found a slug
it's like a zoo round here.

On Sunday mornings Mum and Dad
woken early by the barking
yowling, grunting, squealing, growling
often try to sleep again.

Until we thunder down the stairs
a charging herd of hungry rhino
laughing loudly, wild hyenas
snuffling in our breakfast bowls.

Then they stagger to the door
their faces grey like wrinkled masks
they spit and snarl, whine and bark
'It's like a zoo round here.'

DAVID HARMER

Visitors

    Downstairs
visitors have arrived,
a tribe of relations
I've never seen before.

    Upstairs
I'm away from it all,
alone in my bedroom
with the portable TV.

    Downstairs
they're sipping sherry
and chomping cherry cake.
There's noise, and fuss.

    Upstairs
I can invite my own visitors
anytime I please.
Press a button and...

    here come
Tom and Jerry, the Neighbours,
those Hero Turtle Mutants,
the Pink Panther,
Laurel and Hardy, and more...

    visitors galore!

Downstairs
they're playing cards.
'Cheat!' 'I won!'
Everyone *shouting!*

Upstairs
I switch off the TV
and draw back the curtain.
Visitors! A dozen, a *score!*

Here come
Orion, Taurus,
Leo, Hercules,
Andromeda,
the Man in the Moon, and more…

visitors galore!

WES MAGEE

Cousins

Every evening
when the dark creeps in
like a smothering black cape,
our little family
– Mum, Dad, Brother, Sister, Gogo the Cat and me –
we get together to huddle and cuddle
and keep us each safe.

Every night
when the moon rises like a white saucer,
our little family
– Mum, Dad, Brother, Sister, Gogo the Cat and me –
go to bed in our warm rooms.
We tuck each other in
and sleep safe in green dreams.

But in another land,
when the same dark creeps in,
a broken family in a wild wind
looks to the same moon, red and angry,
and each makes a wish.
– Mum, Dad, Brother, Sister, Asmara the Stray Dog –
all ask for food, for medicine, for peace, for rain.
Just these, only these, do our beautiful cousins ask for.

JOHN RICE

Index of First Lines

Alice hates her sister	43
Aunt Sue has a head full of stories	72
Cosmo's weird and Billy's naughty	11
Dad is the dancing-man	15
Dad says I'm crazy	16
Dad's left. Is that right?	23
Dear Mamma, if you just could be	20
Do put a coat on	60
Downstairs	84
Every evening	86
Father, mother	14
Grandpa's hands are as rough as garden sacks	68
Grow up, girl	12
Harry pushed her	54
I know a girl with thirteen grandmas	65
I like being left alone	55
I'm always doing things wrong	9
It was high summer	80
Jemima is my name	45
Lively Lou and Lazy Lynn	49
Melanie, Melanie Wilberforce	38
Mi baby sista come home las' week	28
Mum says	78
My brother is a punk	30
My dad says	64
My father lied for me	22
My grandpa is as round-shouldered as a question mark	63
My little sister told a lie	52
My mum was a mince pie of a mum	17
My mum's borrowed my mountain bike	10
My sister	46
My sister and I	36
Nineteen-o-nine	64
Now we're siting round the table	74
One cannot turn a minute	39
Our back garden swarms with cats	82

Richard…	31
Sally hasn't talked to me for ages	50
She puts her hands in the sink – with each deft flick	19
Sisters	44
Tell me a story!	48
The cat's got run over	77
The minnows I caught	66
The thing I can't stand	8
There's a place	56
These are the shoes	24
These days I'm in love with my face	59
They say I've got my father's nose	58
This morning	42
Through the house what busy joy	27
Wash yuh han dem before yuh eat	69
We're so different in size	35
'Were you born in a field?'	7
When Daddy was in bed	16
When my cousin Janice	76
When we caught measles	34
Where do aunties come from	70
Who spilled this milk?	13
Why this child	62
William!	40
Wipe! Wipe! Wipe!	32
You really are lucky	26

Index of Poets

Andrew, Moira 52
Bloom, Valerie 28, 69
Bonner, Ann 46
Bradman, Tony 14, 43
Calder, Dave 19
Cook, Stanley 35
Curry, Jennifer & Graeme 11
Dayre, Sydney (Mrs Cochran) 20
de la Mare, Walter 45
Dixon, Peter 17, 64
Doherty, Berlie 15, 68
Douthwaite, Gina 23, 44
Foster, John 8, 78
Gammon, Natasha 16
Gowar, Mick 51
Harmer, David 10, 82
Harvey, Trevor 34
Hughes, Langston 72
Hunt, Leigh 39
Jones, Peter Thabit 54
Lamb, Charles & Mary 27
McCann, Kevin 64
Magee, Wes 66, 80, 84
Mather, Ray 40
Mayer, Gerda 59
Mellor, Robin 26, 65
Millum, Trevor 49, 55
Mole, John 24
Moses, Brian 9, 36
Nicholls, Judith 48, 60
Nichols, Grace 62
Owen, Gareth 58, 76
Rawnsley, Irene 22

Rice, John   13, 86
Sedgwick, Fred   12, 56
Simpson, Matt   7, 38
Souter, Ian   32, 42, 63
Strachan, Desmond   31
Thomson, Charles   30
Webster, Clive   16
Wiley, Martin   70
Yates, Irene   77
Young, Bernard   74

Acknowledgements

The editor and Publisher would like to thank the following for their kind permission to reprint copyright material in this book:

Moira Andrew for 'One thing leads to another'; Valerie Bloom for 'Good Advice' and 'New Baby' from *Another 3rd Poetry Book*, ed John Foster (Oxford University Press, 1988); Ann Bonner for 'My Little Sister'; Rogers, Coleridge and White Ltd for 'Ties' and 'Alice' by Tony Bradman copyright © Tony Bradman; Dave Calder for 'Magic'; Stanley Cook for 'Big and Little'; Methuen Children's Books for 'Wilde by Name' by Jennifer and Graeme Curry from *Down our Street* (Methuen, 1988); The Literary Trustees of Walter de la Mare and the Society of Authors as their representatives for 'Mima' by Walter de la Mare; Peter Dixon for 'My Mum' and 'Grandad's Birthday'; Berlie Doherty for 'Dad' and 'Grandpa' from *Another First Poetry Book* ed John Foster (Oxford University Press, 1987); Gina Douthwaite for 'Divorce' and 'Sisters'; John Foster for 'Early to Bed' and 'It's a Dog's Life'; Macmillan, London and Basingstoke for 'Daddy in Bed' by Natasha Gammon from *Young Words* (Macmillan, 1988); Viking Kestrel for 'Sisters' by Mick Gowar from *Third Time Lucky* (Viking Kestrel, 1988), copyright © 1988 Mick Gowar; David Harmer for 'Lisa's Protest' and 'Wildlife'; Trevor Harvey for 'Favouritism' from *Poetry for Projects* ed Pie Corbett/Brian Moses (Scholastic, 1989); Langston Hughes for 'Aunt Sue's Stories' from *Wheel Around the World* ed Chris Searle (Macdonald, 1983); Cambridge University Press for 'Until Gran Died', 'Gran's Green Parrot' and 'Visitors' by Wes Magee from *Morning Break and other poems*; Ray Mather for 'William'; Gerda Mayer for 'Well Caught'; Kevin McCann for 'Birthdays'; Robin Mellor for 'The New Baby' and 'Thirteen Grandmas'; Trevor Millum for 'Lively Lou and Lazy Lynn' and 'Alone in the House' from *Warning – too much schooling can damage your health* (E J Arnold); Blackie and Son Ltd for 'The Shoes' by John Mole from *Catching the Spider* (Blackie, 1990); Brian Moses for 'This

Time' and 'Face Pulling Contests'; Faber and Faber Ltd for 'Sister' and 'Advice' by Judith Nicholls from *Midnight Forest* (Faber, 1987); Curtis Brown for 'Poor Grandma' by Grace Nichols from *Come on into my Tropical Garden* (A & C Black); Rogers, Coleridge and White Ltd for 'Cousin Janice with the Big Voice' and 'Unfair' by Gareth Owen, copyright © Gareth Owen; Irene Rawnsley for 'Lies'; John Rice for 'The Pleasures of Family Conversation' and 'Our Beautiful Cousins' from *Infant Projects: Families* (Scholastic); Fred Sedgwick for 'Mementoes' and 'Things they say' from *Two by Two* by John Cotton and Fred Sedgwick (Mary Glasgow, 1990); Matt Simpson for 'Enter the Hero' and 'One Spring Day'; Ian Souter for 'Brother Trouble', 'Would you believe it' and 'My Grandpa'; Desmond Strachan for 'Richard's Brother Speaks' from *Another First Poetry Book* ed John Foster (Oxford University Press, 1987); Peter Thabit Jones for 'Harry Pushed Her' from *A Shooting Star*, ed Wes Magee (Blackwell); Charles Thomson for 'My Brother is a Punk'; Clive Webster for 'Crazy'; Martyn Wiley for 'A Mystery'; Irene Yates for 'Nine Down'; Bernard Young for 'Afternoon Tease'.

Every effort has been made to trace the copyright holders but the editor and Publisher apologise if any inadvertent omission has been made.